Praise for *Before the Foundation of the World*

"*Before the Foundation of the World* is poetry of the highest sort. It is a wonderful fusion of artistry and truth. It takes the reader to places where prose cannot go, into the mystery of the spirit where good and evil reside. Susan Weiner has created an enduring Christian testament that speaks to both believer and unbeliever. It is a triumph for her. I feel myself drawn back into her poetry again and again."

—Curtis J. Young, senior pastor,
Church of the Atonement, Silver Spring, MD

"Poetry challenges us to see things in a different way. Susan Weiner's lovely poems lead us to meditate on God's love and greatness, His Son's birth and ultimate sacrifice, and of His mysterious workings in our lives and in the world around us. In these verses, biblical events come alive, urging us to see the stars and the stable, hear the thunder of the stormy seas, feel the sand beneath our feet, smell the spices, taste the honey—and marvel at what God has done for us."

—Anne Morse, author (with Charles Colson) of *Burden of Truth* and
(with Congressman Frank R. Wolf) of *Prisoner of Conscience*

"Like fine cuisine, Susan Weiner's *Before the Foundation of the World* is rich food for the soul not to be devoured hastily, but savored slowly and deliberately. Powerful images engage all the senses, transporting the reader back to biblical times, bringing to life the realities of good and evil and the ultimate victory God has given us in Christ. This is poetry for our time—a beautiful declaration of God's glory and His unfathomable love for His people."

—Joanne Hamilton, former president,
Associate Reformed Presbyterian Women's Ministries

Best Wishes, Susan

BEFORE THE

FOUNDATION

OF THE WORLD

- SUSAN WEINER -

ISBN: 978-1-947860-45-2

LCCN: 2019909647

Design by Michael Hardison
Production management by Christina Kann

Cover illustration: © matorina / Adobe Stock #196184680
Interior illustrations: AlfredoM Graphic Arts Studio

All verses quoted from the Bible have been taken from the New King James Version, except for the verse found on page 15, where the Revised Standard Version is used.

Printed in the United States of America

Published by
Belle Isle Books (an imprint of Brandylane Publishers, Inc.)
5 S. 1st Street
Richmond, Virginia 23219

BELLE ISLE BOOKS
www.belleislebooks.com

belleislebooks.com | brandylanepublishers.com

TABLE OF CONTENTS

Cinnamon and Myrrh

Oh, precious spice of my heart,
What spark of augury or art

Made salient the spell of your soul on me
And traced in golden filigree

The imprint of your name
Through every vein and byway flesh can frame?

Let kings to holy wars raise their name
And sacred sibyls speak of fame;

Let temples fall to desert sands
And trade routes clear of caravans.

Your love, the center stone of my heart,
Of blood and breath has joined each part.

Sorcerers make shadows of all things unsure.
All the days of my life, you bring me cinnamon and myrrh.

Noah and the Dove

In Memoriam Wayne S. Fenton

Like the Euphrates water came down
And beast and man together drowned.

They sank beneath a roaring sea
Mountains crowned could neither flee,

When an angel's sword broke the sky
And death stood by his woeful cry.

Of gopher wood God bade me build,
And two by two that ark was filled,

For a blossom springs to temper grief
And promise lights an olive leaf;

So, a bow will shine across the sea
And hills hold wine and honey.

From chaos see how beauty springs:
The dove above the water sings.

Gloria in Excelsis Deo

Gloria, Gloria in Excelsis, called the Lord
And the mists were hung from bay to fjord,

And the voice of the elk was beside the lake
And the breath of calf came fully awake.

Every tulip tree flowered with the dawn
And the geese rose as pale as the swan:

For *in Gloria* is written the works of God,
Who has cast each hill with staff and rod,

So yellow daffodils spring beneath the sun
And hollyhock from each simple seed is spun.

So, if mountains smoke and lands begin to quake
And raging seas make the heavens start to shake,

If even stars can fall and planets stop their spin,
Still glory will win, and all of grace will conquer sin.

Parthian Wine 1

Your love is better than Parthian wine,
Better than Attic coins where gorgons shine;

Better than caravans that sashay over sands
Whose bells are heard through many lands,

Or courtesans with henna on their hands
Who unveil dark eyes beside the market stands;

Better than oracles who consult with bones to see
And make their fires in juniper to aid in prophecy,

Imperial baths and the flaxen gowns of queens:
Your love is sweeter than a rich man's dreams,

Sweeter than the honey of an Ephesian bee
Or Phoenician holds of timber and ivory,

Because even Xerxes and his siege engines will fall,
And broken lie the temples of Jupiter and Ba'al.

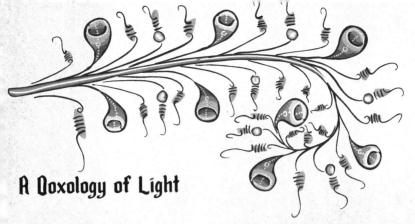

A Doxology of Light

The world is suffused with the glory of light,
Each blowing leaf in the sun is bright.

Each blade of grass bears a coronet of flame
In a kingdom the Spirit will call by name.

Every species on earth is a covenant in fire,
While every oak, every mountain is a spire,

Where the white-tailed deer and the plains gazelle
Graze along grasses within an amber spell.

See how storm clouds give way to rivers of the sun
Where the fields of oats and rye are golden spun,

Because the light that sparkles on the surface of the sea
Is the same that gilds the budding sycamore tree.

Oh, how the glory of God breaks over the earth like a wave:
The light rising, the light shining, the light whose luminance will save.

Joseph in Egypt

Bearer of wheat in a foreign land,
Grain like gold before the desert sand,

As the Nile lay sheathed in gilded leaf
And goat's blood murmured like a thief,

In the shadow of Potiphar and Pharaoh's hand,
You bore the summons of a fiery brand.

For Abraham lit the embers of your dreams
With a love more fair than kohl-eyed queens;

And in a prison bright with angels' wings,
Your fate was bound to crested rings.

In the land of the dead, behold the living God
And see how tender a hand attends the measuring rod,

For as surely as Satan played upon dark strings,
You were held more dear than the emeralds of pharaohs or kings.

Cleopatra, Daughter of Amun-Ra

Do not lay up for yourselves treasures on earth,
where moth and rust destroy and where
thieves break in and steal.   (Matthew 6:19)

Daughter of Amun-Ra, fair as pearls,
Cleopatra among her dancing girls,

Behold the crown of Antony put away
And Egypt burnished bright as day.

Your gold and bronze reflect the fire
Of generals and their martial choir,

Whose fields of blood and empire fall;
And to Cleopatra came the serpent's call.

Oh, Pharaoh, scion of the morning star,
Beware the deep spaces of the Minotaur,

Because the sea is a sibyl of thunder,
A golden throne is weighed for plunder,

And all that was cedar, cinnamon, balm, and myrrh
Will fall to savage gods at your capture.

Parthian Wine II

Your love is brighter than a Roman sword
Or sun on the shields of the Scythian horde;

Greater than kings, barbarous or kind,
Or decrees with bloody sacrifice signed;

Greater than a triumph met with applause
Where leopards go by on golden paws;

Greater than elephants or a fury's steeds,
Descended from creatures of mighty deeds.

Because even as the gates of Babylon fall
And timbers blaze in the emperor's hall,

As luminous as the Colossus of Rhodes,
On fields of souls, you reap what you sowed.

For though men and mountains will surely fail,
There is a kingdom for the throne of Israel.

Ten Thousand Suns

Then Jesus spoke to them again, saying, "I am the light of the world."
(John 8:12)

When photons reigned ten thousand years
And quasars rose with golden spears,

When matter, mass, and math took form
And angels spoke like thundering storm,

You made both space and time belong
And gave the shining stars their song.

When electrons gathered into flight
And stars gave birth to elementary light,

When gravity's well was black as pitch
And galaxies bright beneath its stitch,

The star-bearer called to meek and lowly
By waters that were christened, oh, so holy.

Almighty God, as glorious as ten thousand suns,
How your bright fire through the dark and endless sea runs.

Be Not Far Away

Yea, though I walk through the valley
of the shadow of death,
I will fear no evil. (Psalm 23:4)

Father, be not far away
When the bones in me decay,

When the bitter herb of death
Scalds the tongue with every breath,

When dust and ashes seal my veins
And sorrow beats down like the rain.

Who has the whirlwind in his hand
And rests his crook on promised land?

Be near to me in glory bright,
Whose broad wings lead the blind to sight.

Oh, pillar of fire and Corinthian cloud,
A lesser seed has been plowed.

In blackest mist, in darkest night,
Let my heart be filled with light.

Parthinian Wine III

How lovely is Your tabernacle, O Lord of hosts! My soul longs,
yes, even faints for the courts of the Lord. (Psalm 84: 1-2)

Your love is stronger than usurpers or kings,
Than an adder's tooth, whose fatal sting

Is a feature of palace plots and cunning deceits;
Your love is stronger than a queen's conceits,

Stronger than the poisons prepared by temple priests
To anoint the favored wine at sacred feasts,

Your love is stronger than a gladiator's sword
And the scarlet blood as each spectator roared,

Stronger than talents of gold and a measure of wheat
That launched an invasion by Caesar's fleet.

For greater than the plundering of citizens and kings,
Are the golden courts, where the seraphim sing

Of fire and thunder among a tempest of wings,
Upon the marbled floor where your step rings.

The Song of the Magi

And you shall know the truth, and the truth shall make you free. (John 8:32)

When Mercury to Capricorn made his way
And Earth cast new flowers from her clay,

When Aquarius foretold a blossoming of stars
And spears of gold were hurled by Mars,

Then winged creatures shining bright
Sang songs of love as strong as might.

When the entrails verified omens and signs
Of foreign lands and fragrant wines,

Then our camels stirred upon the sand
And we swayed with gold and spices grand,

And left our gathering of planets and gods
And with scholars and kings became at odds.

For we have seen a child swaddled in light
And are no longer blind and groping in the night.

Emmanuel

I, an ancient king from a far-off land,
Have come across the endless dunes of sand

To bow before shepherds, oxen, and sheep
To a child whose eyes are full of sleep.

Oh, Holy Anointed One of the Lord,
Mashiah, *Christos*, blessed and adored,

May the burning star move swift in flight
To shower on you its raiment of light—

Let even angels lift their glorious wings
Before the tent of the King of Kings.

For you, sweet incense and Nubian gold
And a God neither young, nor ever old.

And now palace lords, oh, sing to me no more,
For here I stand, steadfast, beside a stable door.

Parthinian Wine IV

Your love is greater than golden rings,
Than silver censers or sweet-smelling things;

Greater than any deep-hued pearls
Or a Persian god whose beard has curls.

Like sapphires on a regnant gown,
Your love gleams more than the sultan's crown.

For oh, so much sweeter than dates and the fig,
Than strawberries and the feast-roasted pig,

Finer than every Egyptian wig,
Is faith like a fragrant rosemary sprig.

For greater than all the empires of kings,
Or the ember of an angel's outspread wings,

Is your love that shapes the world anew,
Whose Christ shines everywhere and always true.

Appendix 1

Apocalyptica
A Call and Response Series

The light shines in the darkness,
and the darkness has not overcome it. (John 1:5)

Pater Mendaciorum 1

Though I speak with the tongue of men and angels, but have not love.
(1 Corinthians 13:1)

I was brighter than the morning sun,
And I paced the stars on their evening run.

I rose with archangels before principalities and lords,
And thousands cried in ravaging chords.

For I spew venom and worship only fire,
And the smoke of my toil rises higher

Than even the towers of men dare to aspire.
Oh, my angels, beat your wings in a dark choir,

For I have taken and twisted the work of his hands:
Blasted are the plains and withered are his lands.

I will make of Man a co-heir;
I will sow hatred at the heart of that tare

And strike so the diamond in his soul is flawed.
Who now can reconcile us to God?

Jesus of Galilee
For Lent

And the Lord has laid on Him the iniquity of us all. (Isaiah 53:6)

Jesus of Galilee: Lord of the Jews,
Christened in blood, with Judas untrue,

Forsaken by Man, before God denied,
To the lash and the thorn become as a bride.

As nails scored both flesh and bone
And dice beneath the cross were thrown,

Then darkness spread across the land
And vultures wheeled above the sand.

So that which was spoken came to be:
Jesus pierced for our iniquity.

Scorned by a crowd, mocked by a jeer,
When water fell from the edge of a spear,

In the place of skulls, in the place of bones,
The son of Mary died alone.

Pater Mendaciorum II

I come, cast in shadows by the light;
I teem with infestation in my bite.

In my hands I crush a delicate soul,
For I am the seal to loose the blackened scroll.

As my heart races before the raging fire,
So, I gnash my teeth in the presence of my sire:

For I, who have wrestled with He Who is Most High,
Am the one for whom the demons sigh.

I will crouch in the dark recesses of your heart
And of your every weakness make a chart,

Because I, who have stepped on holy ground unshod,
Will forever keep you from the face of God,

I, who will never know again what it is to be whole;
I, who bore the brightened hem of Jesus's stole.

The Apocalypse

Now I saw a new heaven and a new earth, for the first heaven
and the first earth had passed away. (Revelation 21:1)

In Jerusalem, shine the light and let the loud trumpets sound,
By the banks of the Euphrates, turn loose the dark angels bound;

See, the clouds are torn through with brimstone, lightning, and hail,
Under bones, the hearts of the wicked tremble and they fail.

Because the Lamb, the Lamb is come, and broken is his seal,
Throw down your wealth and give away what you steal.

For the Lamb, the Lamb comes beyond fire and blood,
When old dominions sway and crumble to mud.

Because the Lamb, the Lamb who was felled by the sword,
Has risen from flesh our Savior, our Lord.

And thunderheads roll with voices, wheels, and Death's piercing call;
The stars tremble in their circuits, and in thousands they fall.

Behold! The dwelling place of God is always and forever with Man.
Let reign on Earth once more God's divine, defining plan.

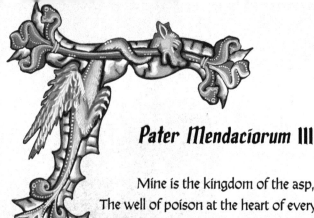

Pater Mendaciorum III

Mine is the kingdom of the asp,
The well of poison at the heart of every wasp.

I am present in the bacchanal of the wine;
With temple whores I scrawl on walls the sign

That I am come to greet the gladness of your days
And steal the golden crown of your Savior's ways.

I am the locust and the swollen dead in every flood,
I am a thousand flies and a flux of flowering blood,

I am the plague whose borders are not found,
And prince to those who lie still and mangled on the ground.

Come and I will make you an empire of the sun,
Black as the hyena, of the horned scorpion stung.

Come, yes, come to me, for I am of hate undimmed
And I hold, just for you, the wild and roaring wind.

I Am Never Far Away

Here am I before the wind that knows my name;
I am the blossom that shimmers like a tongue of flame.

I am the voice of bells that sweetens morning's breeze;
I am the spoken word that shapes the leaf on trees.

In my hands, vast infinity exploded into light,
And I loosed the sphere a sun would capture in its flight.

One day, neutrons, protons, atomic nuclei, and quarks
Seized and bound me in their subtle web of arcs;

And so, I was raised on the transverse of a cross,
Triumphant over iron nails to rescue you from loss.

Believe in me for I am the Resurrection, the Word, the Narrow Way.
The peace I keep for you is confirmed in a tulip's spring display.

Let the fishes and the beasts herald the breaking of my day,
For, just as sunlight speckles morning's foal, I am never far away.

Pater Mendaciorum IU

*Because your adversary the devil
walks about like a roaring lion,
seeking whom he may devour. (1 Peter 5:8)*

In igni voranti, I defile myself.
I am come with wrath athwart the gulf.

Loving creation I cannot suffer,
But I can rend the soul in its coffer.

In omnino inani Spiritus Sancti
The dead will rise to see,

At the living God I bare my teeth
And wear my wicked soul like a winner's wreath;

Of pestilence I make my renown;
With the cities of Sodom I shape my crown.

Promise the slaves dough without leaven,
Imprecor maledicta firmamento of Heaven.

I am he who stands at the beginning too.
Creatus e meipso, in tenebris, I am new.

The Rose

There shall come forth a Rod from the stem of Jesse,
and a Branch shall grow from out of his roots. (Isaiah 11:1)

From the earth, where the lowly worm grows,
To the grave, where the black crow goes,

In the deep and silent heart of the loam,
Where the blind moles scratch and the pale grubs roam,

Where mushrooms are situated like a crown
And the scent of carrion is sweet renown,

There is a root that cannot be found,
Cannot be measured or pulled from the ground—

Whose thorn-tipped stem is risen like spring
Among scarlet fruits and the blossoming,

Whose fair green leaves are luminous to a light
The powdery mildew cannot brush with blight:

Greater than dusk and the fluttering moth, behold the Rose,
As brighter than the Northern Star its flower grows.

Appendix 2

Encomia

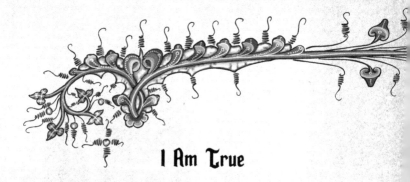

I Am True

When I scattered stars like coals shining bright
And comets rose like a swallow's flight,

When the rings about Saturn were formed
And the belly of the earth was warmed,

Then I had a plan for you, a plan for you.
No matter how far you fall, I will be true.
No matter how far you fall, I will be true.

When the morning stars sang in sweet harmony
And the ocean's swell was a symphony,

When a garden shone with marvelous flower
And two knew the virtue of their early hour,

Then I had a plan for you, a plan for you.
No matter how far you fall, I will be true.
No matter how far you fall, I will be true.

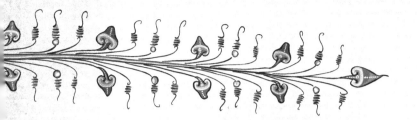

When the moons about Jupiter split
And the warp of space loosed its knit,

When sin knocked the orbit of the sun undone
And a web of galaxies came unspun,

Still I had a plan for you, a plan for you.
No matter how far you fall, I will be true.
No matter how far you fall, I will be true.

When I lay a veil on the palace of the sun
And a man at Calvary was undone,

When the Temple curtain tore in two,
Then was shed My Grace for you, My Grace for you.

For I have had a plan for you, for all time a plan for you.
No matter how far you fall, I am true.
No matter how far you fall, I am true.

The Hymn of the Magi

The people who walked in darkness have seen a great light. (Isaiah 9:2)

Verse 1
In Bethlehem, a city too small for emperors or kings,
Glad tidings of a virgin's birth we bring.

For lo, a star that shone so marvelous and bright
Led us through the desert, through the shadow of the night.

And the constellations broke beneath the radiant light,
While angels sang with fires, like torches in my sight.

Chorus
Singing grace to God the Father and to the Holy One,
For unto Man is given salvation in a Son.

With ears you will hear, with eyes you can see
That they who dwell in darkness shall be free.

Verse 2

And on the manger boards, upon the straw of beasts,
There lay a child who counted with the least,

And still every shepherd left their flock to see
This boy we adored on our bended knees.

Oh, son of Israel, Jerusalem's prince, and great Earth's king,
Glad tidings of you, glad tidings we bring.

Chorus

Singing grace to God the Father and to the Holy One,
For unto Man is given salvation in a Son.

With ears you will hear, with eyes you can see
That they who dwell in darkness shall be free.

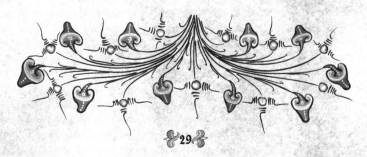

Lullaby 1

What glories are done in your name,
The magnolia spreads your fame.

The deer and alder show your flame,
A storm-wracked sea will grow tame

And thunders still beneath your aim,
So glories are done in your name.

What glories are done in your name,
The scarlet hills reveal the claim

Of the sun's unyielding flame,
The lion with the lamb falls tame

Through him who shines on each the same,
So glories are done in your name.

What glories are done in your name,
The water lily conveys your aim

And unfolds each leaf aflame,
The earth delights beneath your claim.

Each fawn and flower extol your fame,
So glories are done in your name.

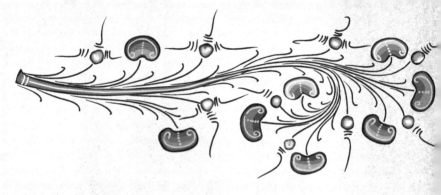

Lullaby II

Chorus 1
Diamonds, rubies, pearls, and gold
And finest laces will be sold.

Dainties sweet and feasts for a king,
Will eyes see only the glittering?

Verses 1–2
Frankincense, myrrh, and fragrant balms,
Do you cry for them as if for alms?

Jasper, carnelian, sapphires, and pearls,
Have you come to see the lords and earls?

Frankincense, myrrh, and fragrant balms,
A soul is more than coins in palms.

Jasper, carnelian, sapphires, and pearls,
A soul is more than sparkling jewels.

Chorus 2

Diamonds, rubies, pearls, and gold
In whose spell, a heart grows cold.

Velvets, silks, and taffetas sing,
Will eyes see only the glimmering?

Verses 3–4

Give frankincense, myrrh, and fragrant balms
For a child among the straw and palms.

He is jasper, carnelian, sapphires, and pearls
Among angels with their wings unfurled.

Give frankincense, myrrh, and fragrant balms,
For nails will pierce his feet and palms.

Give jasper, carnelian, sapphires, and pearls,
His grace will spread across the world.

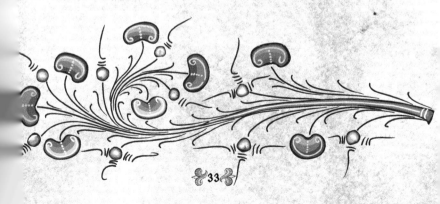

Lullaby III

Oh, give me not gold,
Nor bright shiny rings.
Please give me no gems
Or pearls on a string.

Oh, give me not dreams
Of gilt-covered things,
Of gowns made of silk
That money may bring.

But give me your love
Like fair buds of spring.
Yes, give me your love
The way nightingales sing.

Oh, give me not toffees,
Nor truffles with cream.
Oh, bring me no chocolates
With centers that gleam.

Of pâtés and caviar,
Of dumplings that steam,
It's only what wealth
And fancy might dream.

But give me your love,
The sun's fiery beam.
Yes, give me your love
Like a tumbling stream.

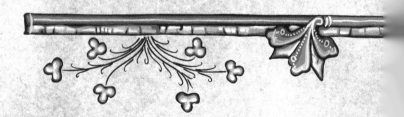

For nothing's like God's love,
His sun's golden ray.
No, nothing's like God's love,
That breaks like the day.

May God shine before you
Like the flowers of May,
And his love fall upon you
As the rain of midday.

Oh, give me your great love,
A horse's sweet neigh,
So splendid an opulence
That won't rot away.

35

Armageddon

Wait upon the coming of the glory of the Lord.
Golden is the blade of his bright and burning sword.
A spreading flame to assemble a lost and scattered horde,
When shining are the shields of the armies of the Lord.

Before his trumpet shall crumble the fortress of the night.
Sin will quake and tremble before the advent of his light.
A host of angels will accompany the cherubim in flight,
When Jesus sets his hand against the cities of the night.

Chorus
See stars and comets falling from the sky,
The ocean's coastal waters running dry,
Broken towers that dared once rise so high,
Before the Lord, whose kingdom cannot die.

Beside his throne, angels shield their eyes with wings,
For he is like the sun upon the golden halls of kings,
Clothed in the glory that redemption brings.
With a word the seraphim unleash their mighty wings.

So, the Messiah comes back for us in chariots of fire;
And his mountains shall ascend like a church's spire,
And the voice of his valleys will be the sound of Heaven's choir,
And the Earth shall bear his glory upon its track of fire.

Chorus:
See stars and comets falling from the sky,
The ocean's coastal waters running dry,
Broken towers that dared once rise so high,
Before the Lord, whose kingdom cannot die.

Acknowledgements

I would like thank my editor, Christina Kann, for her skillful attention to detail and thoughtful answers to all my questions. Working with her on our second project has been an inestimable delight. Many thanks are due to Michael Hardison for his great talent in the design and layout that have graced my pages. He not only listened to me but also exceeded my hopes. And as always, to Robert Pruett, my deepest thanks for choosing to work with me. I am grateful for this opportunity.

Susan Weiner completed her undergraduate studies in English literature in England and America. She matriculated to UCLA to study seventeenth-century English history in graduate school. Following her education in secular institutions, she found enduring Christian faith as an adult. As a writer, her love of God informed this book, dedicated to sharing the good news of the Messiah and examining the nature of good and evil in the world. Susan lives in Maryland, next to a farm. She spends time in her study, overlooking a herd of deer grazing in the fields. You may see more of her work or contact her at www.susanweinerbooks.com.

CPSIA information can be obtained
at www.ICGtesting.com
Printed in the USA
BVHW090111120919
558233BV00004B/19/P